# GARBAGE TRUCKS

by Marlene Targ Brill

Lerner Publications Company • Minneapolis

*To RBB, who loves anything that takes away garbage—mtb*

*The author wishes to thank Tom Foleno from Onyx Waste Service, who answered lots of questions for this book.*

Text copyright © 2005 by Marlene Targ Brill

All rights reserved. International copyright secured. No part of this book may be reproduced, stored in a retrieval system, or transmitted in any form or by any means—electronic, mechanical, photocopying, recording, or otherwise—without the prior written permission of Lerner Publishing Group, Inc., except for the inclusion of brief quotations in an acknowledged review.

This book is available in two editions:
Library binding by Lerner Publications Company, a division of Lerner Publishing Group, Inc.
Soft cover by First Avenue Editions, an imprint of Lerner Publishing Group, Inc.
241 First Avenue North
Minneapolis, MN 55401 U.S.A.

Website address: www.lernerbooks.com

Words in **bold type** are explained in a glossary on page 30.

Library of Congress Cataloging-in-Publication Data

Brill, Marlene Targ.
    Garbage trucks / by Marlene Targ Brill.
      p.  cm. — (Pull ahead books)
    Summary: Describes a garbage truck used to dump garbage in a landfill as well as a truck that carries garbage that can be recycled.
      ISBN-13: 978-0-8225-1539-5 (lib. bdg. : alk. paper)
      ISBN-10: 0-8225-1539-3 (lib. bdg. : alk. paper)
      ISBN-13: 978-0-8225-2381-9 (pbk. : alk. paper)
      ISBN-10: 0-8225-2381-7 (pbk. : alk. paper)
      1. Refuse collection vehicles—Juvenile literature.
    [1. Refuse collection vehicles. 2. Trucks.] I. Title.
    II. Series.
    TD794.B74 2005
    628.4'42—dc22                2003022166

Manufactured in the United States of America
3 – BP – 5/1/12

What happens to **garbage** that you throw out?

A garbage truck picks it up. Garbage trucks carry away things you don't want.

They dump the garbage in a landfill.
A **landfill** is a big hole in the ground
for garbage.

HONK!  HONK!  Here comes the garbage truck now.

The front of the truck is called the **cab**.
A driver sits inside the cab.

SCREECH! The driver stops the truck
by the first garbage can.

The driver gets out to load the garbage
into the truck.  Where does he put all
the bags?

PLOP! PLOP! The driver throws garbage bags into the back of the truck.

The back of the truck is called the
**hopper.** How will the driver lift large
garbage cans into the hopper?

Large garbage cans hook onto the truck.  The driver pulls a **lever** on the side of the truck.

12

The garbage can is lifted up. What happens to the garbage from the can?

KERPLUNK! KERPLUNK! Garbage
drops into the hopper.

Then the driver moves the truck to the next garbage can.  How does one truck hold garbage from so many cans?

The driver pushes another lever on the side of the truck. This lever moves a big **blade.**

The blade slides along the hopper floor
like a moving wall. It crushes the
garbage. Now even more garbage fits
in the truck.

Some trucks
load garbage
from the side.

Others load from the front. YUCK! Garbage trucks stink from all the smelly garbage! Where do the trucks go when they are full?

# Full trucks take their load to a landfill.

# Does all garbage go to a landfill?

Many towns **recycle** some garbage.
Special garbage trucks called
**recycling trucks** take this garbage
to factories.

Recycling trucks have different boxes inside. Drivers throw paper in one box and glass and cans in another.

Workers at factories sort the paper, glass, and cans.

They turn garbage into new things.
Recycled garbage can become toys or
boxes or jars.

Cities and towns need garbage trucks
to take their garbage away.

VRR-OOM! VRR-OOM! Make way for the garbage truck!

# Facts About Garbage Trucks

- The first garbage trucks were carts pulled by horses.

- A garbage truck weighs as much as five elephants.

- Small trucks load their garbage onto bigger trucks at a station. The big trucks take garbage to a landfill.

- Each truck can pick up garbage at 400 to 500 homes per load.

- Every family in the United States throws away about 45 pounds of garbage each week. That's enough garbage to fill 63,000 garbage trucks. Picture the line of garbage trucks needed for one year. The line would stretch from Earth halfway to the moon.

# Parts of a Garbage Truck

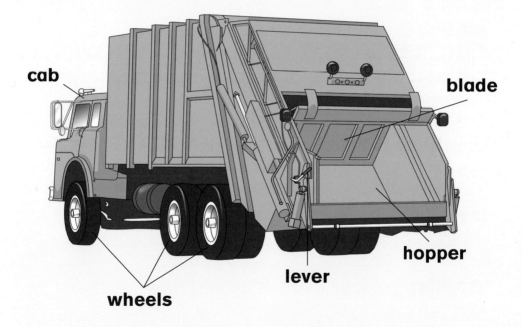

cab

blade

wheels

lever

hopper

# Glossary

**blade:** a part of the truck that slides along the hopper floor and crushes garbage

**cab:** the front of the truck where the driver sits

**garbage:** things people throw away

**hopper:** the part of a garbage truck that holds garbage

**landfill:** a big hole in the ground where garbage trucks dump their loads

**lever:** the handle that drivers pull to move the blade or to lift garbage cans into the hopper

**recycle:** to make into something new

**recycling trucks:** trucks that take garbage to factories to be remade and used again

# Index

# About the Author

Marlene Targ Brill loves to learn how things work. For this book, she watched workers pick up garbage behind her Illinois home. She talked with people who sell trucks and others who recycle garbage. She asked them questions about their jobs. Their answers turned into the story in this book.

## Photo Acknowledgments

The photographs in this book appear courtesy of: © Mack Trucks, Inc./Department of Energy/National Renewable Energy Laboratory, cover; © Jeff Greenberg/Visuals Unlimited, pp. 3, 26; © Erin Liddell/Independent Picture Service, pp. 4, 7, 13, 19; © Inga Spence/Visuals Unlimited, p. 5; © Todd Strand/Independent Picture Service, pp. 6, 12, 15, 16, 17, 31; © John Sohlden/Visuals Unlimited, p. 8; © David H. Wells/CORBIS, p. 9; © Frank M. Hanna/Visuals Unlimited, p. 10; © Warren Gretz/Department of Energy/National Renewable Energy Laboratory, p. 11; © James Alan Brown/Visuals Unlimited, p. 14; © Brokaw/Visuals Unlimited, p. 18; © Courtesy of Environmental Protection Agency, p. 20; © PhotoDisc Royalty Free by Getty Images, pp. 21, 27; © Mark E. Gibson/Visuals Unlimited, p. 22; © Hank Andrews/Visuals Unlimited, p. 23; © Craig Hammell/CORBIS, p. 24; © Joseph Sohm; ChromoSohm, Inc./CORBIS, p. 25.